WALKING WITH DINOSAURS
THE 3D MOVIE

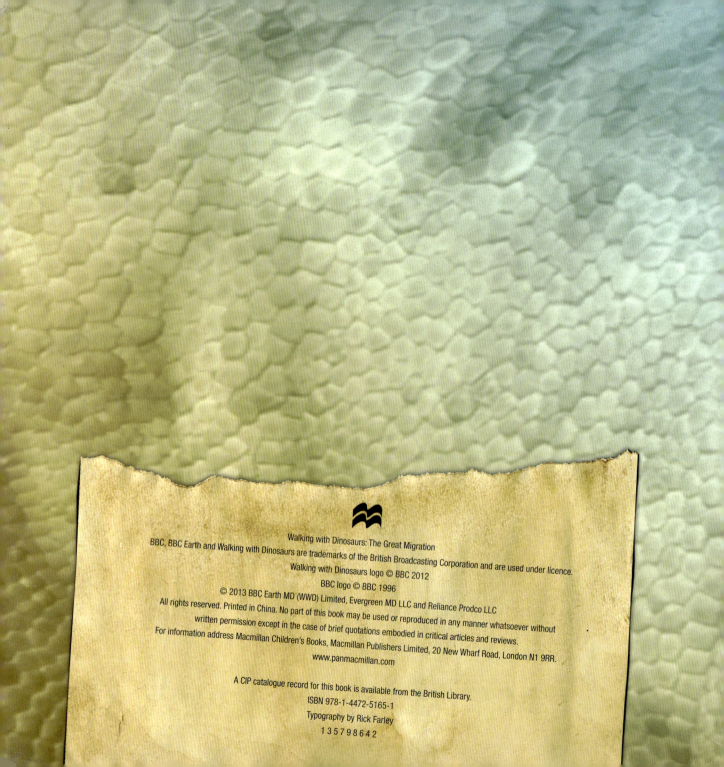

Walking with Dinosaurs: The Great Migration

BBC, BBC Earth and Walking with Dinosaurs are trademarks of the British Broadcasting Corporation and are used under licence.

Walking with Dinosaurs logo © BBC 2012

BBC logo © BBC 1996

© 2013 BBC Earth MD (WWD) Limited, Evergreen MD LLC and Reliance Prodco LLC

For information address Macmillan Children's Books, Macmillan Publishers Limited, 20 New Wharf Road, London N1 9RR.

www.panmacmillan.com

A CIP catalogue record for this book is available from the British Library.

ISBN 978-1-4472-5165-1

Typography by Rick Farley

1 3 5 7 9 8 6 4 2

WALKING WITH DINOSAURS
THE 3D MOVIE

The Great Migration

Adapted by J. E. Bright

MACMILLAN CHILDREN'S BOOKS

Millions of years ago, a new group of hatchlings was born in the Pachyrhinosaurus nesting ground. Scowler was the oldest hatchling. He was much stronger and bigger than all his brothers and sisters, especially his youngest brother, Patchi.

As they grew, Patchi and Scowler often played together. Even though Scowler always won when they wrestled, Patchi never gave up!

Their father, Bulldust, was the leader of the Pachyrhinosaurus herd. Bulldust and Scowler could do many things together because Scowler was big and tough.

Patchi joined them whenever he could.

One day, Patchi followed a butterfly into the woods. He stopped to drink at a pond. There he saw the reflection of another young Pachyrhinosaurus. This was Juniper. Patchi wanted to be her friend, but her mother led her away.

When summer began to fade, Bulldust prepared
the herd to migrate south before the weather turned cold.
Bulldust led his family and the rest of the herd
of Pachyrhinosaurus into the woods as a terrible
thunderstorm gathered overhead.

Lightning hit a tree, starting an enormous forest fire. Many of the dinosaurs panicked and fled.

Suddenly, a Gorgosaurus appeared in the woods near Scowler and Patchi. Bulldust bellowed a warning to his sons.

Patchi and Scowler ran, but a burning tree fell behind them. They were separated from the rest of the herd.
The Gorgosaurus cornered them.

Patchi and Scowler escaped the fire and the Gorgosaurus, but they couldn't find their family, or the rest of the herd.

By the time the fire died down, the whole forest was destroyed. Patchi and Scowler watched the dinosaurs that passed them, but they were all strangers.

Suddenly, Patchi recognized a young Pachyrhinosaurus. It was Juniper!
Delighted, Patchi raced over to Juniper and her mother. Scowler followed along.
Patchi and Scowler followed Juniper and her mother away from the burned forest.
All around them, thousands of different dinosaurs were travelling the same way.

The enormous migration of dinosaurs reached a green valley. They fed on the plants and rested until a pack of Gorgosaurus attacked!

The dinosaurs panicked and tried to escape. Patchi, Scowler and Juniper were pushed along in a wild stampede!

Juniper and the brothers were separated from Juniper's mother. They were shoved towards a cliff above a raging river.

As the Gorgosaurus attacked again, Patchi, Scowler and Juniper fell into the river! The rushing water whisked them downstream.

The three young Pachyrhinosaurus struggled against the strong current, washing up on a foggy beach. Juniper had hurt her leg.

Now the three young dinosaurs were lost. How could they get back to the migration?
A group of enormous, plant-eating Edmontosaurus stomped past, and Patchi, Scowler and Juniper decided to follow them.

Juniper couldn't keep up with the Edmontosaurus because of her hurt leg. Patchi stayed with her, while Scowler vanished in the mists up ahead.

Patchi and Juniper made their way slowly down the beach, and eventually turned back into the forest.

Deep in the woods, a group of dinosaurs called Chirostenotes attacked Juniper and Patchi.

Patchi had had enough of being pushed around! He fought back, defending Juniper from the Chirostenotes.

All the noise attracted a fearsome Gorgosaurus. He found them in the woods but he went after the Chirostenotes while Patchi and Juniper escaped.

Finally, they reached the edge of the forest, where a strange green light filled the night sky. Patchi and Juniper gazed down into a huge valley.

Below them were thousands of grazing dinosaurs. They had found the Winter Ground! Juniper's mother and Scowler were there along with the rest of the Pachyrhinosaurus herd.

Patchi, Scowler and Juniper had made it through the Great Migration. They were safe for the winter. But the young Pachyrhinosaurus would make the journey from the nesting ground to the Winter Ground many times throughout their lives. And one day, Scowler and Patchi both hoped to lead the herd on the Great Migration.